BASICS

MASONRY
CONSTRUCTION

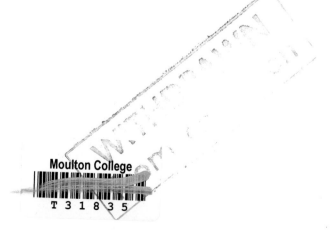

\\ NILS KUMMER

BASICS

MASONRY CONSTRUCTION

BIRKHÄUSER – PUBLISHERS FOR ARCHITECTURE
BASEL·BOSTON·BERLIN

CONTENTS

FOREWORD

"The brick is another master-teacher. How profound that little format is, handy, how useful for every purpose. What logic its structure shows in bond. How lively is that play of joints. And what richness even the simplest area of wall possesses. But what discipline this material demands."

What Ludwig Mies van der Rohe (1886–1969), one of the most influential artists of the 20th century and the last director of the Dessau Bauhaus, is enthusiastically celebrating here is nothing other than one of the lowest common denominators and at the same time essential basic elements of any architecture: masonry. It appears in so many different forms that it is scarcely possible to provide a complete survey. Whether you look at ancient amphitheatres, Babylonian temples, modern museums or simple houses: without bare brick combined with simple mortar, architecture as we know it today can scarcely be explained.

But the well-nigh infinite creative variety afforded by masonry conceals strict rules that have to be obeyed if the desired overall impression is to be guaranteed. The pathway from the brick to the wall, to the room and finally to the whole building is neither short nor simple.

The "Basics" series of books aims to present information didactically and in a form appropriate to practice. It will introduce students to the various specialist fields of training in architecture. Content is developed stage by stage, using readily understandable introductions and explanations. The essential points of departure are built up systematically and explored further in the individual volumes. The concept is not to provide a comprehensive collection of expert knowledge, but to introduce the subject, explain it, and provide the necessary expertise for skilled implementation.

The present volume aims to introduce students systematically to the subject of masonry. Bricks and mortar, the elemental basic components, are used to devise rules for building a wall. The emphasis is on the overall systems and material-dependent properties that are essential for understanding a "wall". The interplay of bricks, the forms of masonry bonds, and the aesthetic of masonry walls with apertures, projections and recesses are explained soundly and methodically – from brick to wall – so that students can understand the essence of masonry and apply their insights directly to their designs and projects.

Bert Bielefeld
Editor

INTRODUCTION

Masonry buildings cannot be reduced to any particular tradition, fashion or style: timeless in their flexibility, fundamental to both classical and avant-garde architecture, open to stylistic trends throughout the ages, capable of being both ordinary and experimental. The façades of contemporary high-rise buildings and modern glass structures may manage without classical masonry as a basic architectural principle, but it is difficult to find buildings without a masonry wall somewhere inside, thus reconfirming the existential character of masonry.

The book will present the "Basics" of masonry, together with the demands it makes. First of all we need to look at its basic components, bricks and mortar. The rules for fitting these elements together to make a wall form the theoretical and creative basis in the second chapter for understanding the wall constructions explained in the third. Then, moving from plain brick construction to the completed wall, we arrive in the fourth chapter at the question of which building materials are suitable for the types of work described earlier, thus ending up with the brick again.

MASONRY
Masonry is not a building material like wood or steel, but a combination of two individual materials, bricks and mortar, handled according to the rules of a craft. It is frequently classified as a composite material, and thus more like reinforced concrete than concrete, for example, as the quality of the end product depends on the quality of both the materials and the execution.

Masonry is used primarily for constructing walls, as a loadbearing or partitioning shear wall, as facing to protect or clad, or as infilling between columns and beams. Bricks are also found in vaults or coping, and also as a floor covering.

There are different kinds of bricks and mortar for all these functions and structures. It is therefore important to know the most important properties of the two materials as well as about construction, so that the ideal combination can be achieved.

THE BRICK
Asked about bricks, most people would probably sketch a uniform shape and size: the standard brick. Developed over millennia, bricks lend

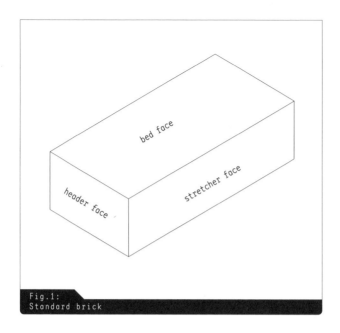

Fig.1:
Standard brick

their character to most masonry façades and are firmly linked with our idea of masonry. But there are a whole variety of different shapes and sizes: flat Roman bricks, large manufactured blocks or octagonal moulded bricks. And the brick forms the basis for the whole set of craft rules of erecting a masonry building, even today. These rules govern the size of rooms and buildings, apertures and built-in features, and they structure façades.

MORTAR FOR MASONRY

The second component of masonry is mortar. It enables the bricks to cover a full area, balances tolerances and ensures that the bricks will hold together strongly, and its finish and colouring influence the look of exposed masonry. It is applied both horizontally between the individual layers of bricks (course joint) and vertically between the individual bricks (perpend). Even though modern manufacturing methods are shrinking the layers of mortar for reasons of cost and structural engineering technology, the combination of brick and mortar is crucial when planning construction. The cohesion of mortar and brick, and thus also the choice of individual components, are important in terms of loadbearing capacity, so that even modern building methods without mortar follow rules based on traditional building.

RULES OF CONSTRUCTION

As masonry is a craft, there are certain rules for achieving a high-quality finish. The most important aims are:

_ Optimizing the loadbearing and resistance properties of the construction
_ Minimizing loss of material
_ Speeding up the building process
_ Executing a design that does justice to material and use

These rules form a theoretical basis for the wall structures given in the third chapter. They show the principles and methods for creating masonry from its components, the preferred dimensions, and how to form connections and apertures correctly for the material. The individual wall will be considered first.

DIMENSIONS AND MODULES
One of the architect's main tasks when planning and constructing a building is to coordinate and combine the various structural and craft services. Shell construction (walls, columns, floors etc.) and finishing (windows, doors, wall and floor coverings etc.) have to be matched in order to build efficiently. The actual building process, as well as planning and finishing, are simplified by repeating elements and sizes. However, fixing grid dimensions is problematical for masonry, as it is impossible to work with the dimensions of the bricks alone, since we must allow for the mortar joints between the bricks as well. Here, a simple device is used to decide when the joint must be added to a wall length or not: the distinction between specified and nominal dimensions.

Specified
dimension and
nominal
dimension

The specified dimension is the basic theoretical measurement, the grid or the module multiplied to put together the whole masonry construction system. The nominal dimension, however, is the dimension that is actually executed and entered on the construction drawing. This distinction can be used to systematize construction types with joints, and particularly masonry constructions.

Although the nominal and specified dimensions are identical when building without joints, they are treated as follows in construction for building types with joints:

11

The specified dimension consists of the nominal dimension executed and the corresponding joint, i.e.:

brick dimension + joint

Conversely, the nominal dimension is the brick dimension alone, without joint.

If you now imagine a masonry wall with window apertures and transverse walls, you will very quickly realize that there are different dimensions for the wall width, aperture and projections because of the mortar joints.

External
dimension

The external dimension is the wall thickness. One joint must always be subtracted from the specified dimension as there is always one joint missing, regardless of the number of bricks.

External dimension (E) = specified dimension – joint

Aperture
dimension

The interior dimension of an aperture always contains an additional joint.

Aperture dimension (A) = specified dimension + joint

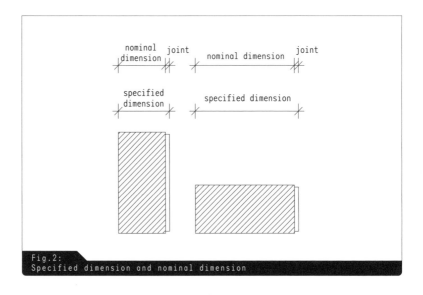

Fig.2:
Specified dimension and nominal dimension

The projection dimension measures the piece of wall between opening and wall or wall projections. Here, the missing joint in the external dimension and the additional joint in the aperture dimensions balance each other out.

Projection dimension (A) = specified dimension

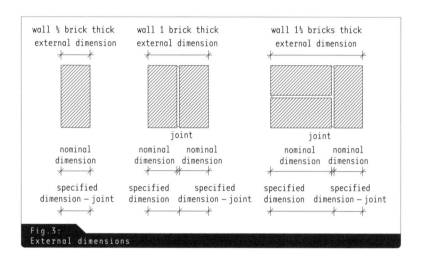

Fig.3:
External dimensions

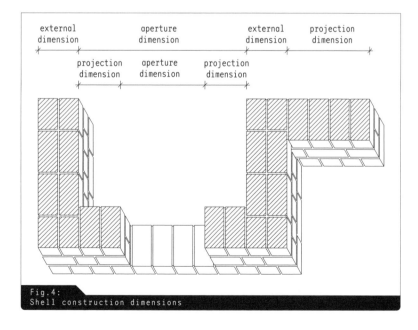

Fig.4:
Shell construction dimensions

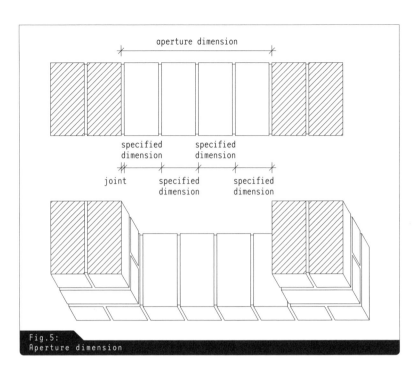

Fig.5:
Aperture dimension

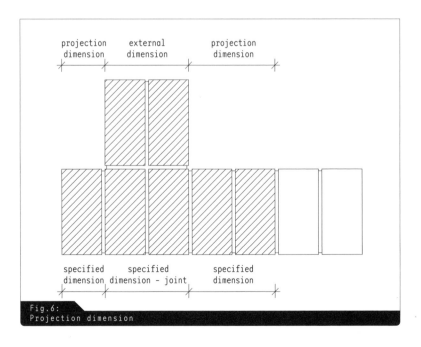

Fig.6:
Projection dimension

UNIT DIMENSIONS AND DESIGNATIONS

These hitherto theoretical definitions have left open the question of actual dimensions, which are independent of the brick and joint sizes chosen. These sizes can vary, and have led to different standards in different countries, according to local traditions.

In Germany, masonry is based almost exclusively on the octametric system, which uses an eighth of a metre = 12.5 cm as the specified dimension. The standard brick, so-called "normal format", measures $24 \times 11 \times 7.1$ cm (nominal dimensions). When the joint sizes for of 1 cm for the vertical head joints and 1.23 cm for the horizontal course joints are added, this gives specified dimensions of $25 \times 12.5 \times 8.33$ cm, multiples of which produce a metre.

Joint sizes can also vary, without changing the system. New manufacturing technology and the need to meet the greater-than-ever demands on masonry for heat and sound insulation, and in terms of loadbearing capacity, mean that masonry technique is no longer based on the centimetre joint. Modern manufactured blocks are finished to such low tolerances that joints need be only a few millimetres thick.

However, to maintain the usual specified dimensions, the unit dimensions have been adapted to ensure that the overall dimensions still fit in with the system:

For example:

Traditional:	German normal format brick	24 cm + 1 cm joint = 25 cm
Modern technique:	Manufactured block	24.7 cm + 3 mm joint = 25 cm

\\ Tip:
In Germany, these dimensions are fixed by the DIN 4172 standard dimension in the building industry, which has prescribed a basic module of 25 cm for shell construction since the post-Second World War rebuilding, basing itself on traditional formats. The later DIN 18000 modular standard for building, which promised to be simpler to use with its decimetric basic module of M – 10 cm, has not caught on in Germany.

\\ Hint:
Different countries have other standard bricks, based on national traditions or different units (e.g. inches), e.g. $21.5 \times 10.25 \times 6.5$ cm in England, $19 \times 9 \times 6.5$ cm in Belgium, and $8 \times 4 \times 2.25$ inches $(20.3 \times 10.2 \times 5.7$ cm) in the USA.

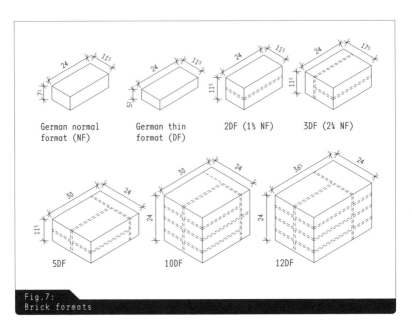

German normal format (NF)

German thin format (DF)

2DF (1½ NF)

3DF (2½ NF)

5DF

10DF

12DF

Fig.7:
Brick formats

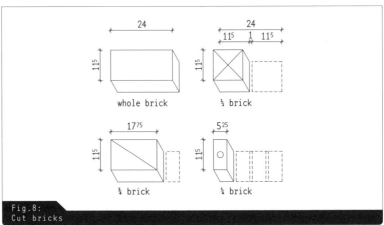

whole brick

½ brick

¾ brick

¼ brick

Fig.8:
Cut bricks

\\ Hint:
As the same number of thin-format units
can be combined in different ways, different
formats produce the same designation, e.g.
8DF = 24 × 24 × 23.8 cm and 8DF = 24 × 49 × 11.3 cm.

16

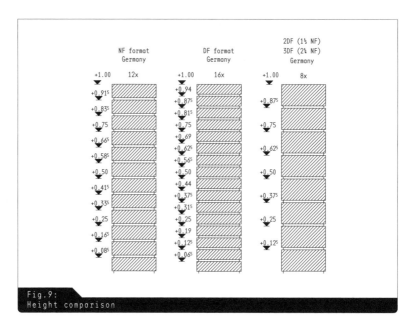

NF format Germany	DF format Germany	2DF (1½ NF) 3DF (2½ NF) Germany
+1.00 12x	+1.00 16x	+1.00 8x
+0.91⁵	+0.94	
+0.83⁵	+0.87⁵	+0.87⁵
+0.75	+0.81⁵	
+0.66⁵	+0.75	+0.75
+0.58⁵	+0.69	
+0.50	+0.62⁵	+0.62⁵
+0.41⁵	+0.56⁵	
+0.33⁵	+0.50	+0.50
+0.25	+0.44	
+0.16⁵	+0.37⁵	+0.37⁵
+0.08⁵	+0.31⁵	
	+0.25	+0.25
	+0.19	
	+0.12⁵	+0.12⁵
	+0.06⁵	

Fig.9:
Height comparison

Small formats are also distinguished:

$L \times W \times H = 24 \times 11.5 \times 7.1$ cm – normal format (NF)
$24 \times 11.5 \times 5.2$ cm – thin format (DF)

Larger bricks are made up of several thin formats as a basic module with the corresponding joints, and are thus defined as 5DF, for example.

Examples for dimensions in the octametric system:

Specified dimensions: 12.5 cm; 25 cm; 37.5 cm; 50 cm ... 100 cm etc.
Nominal dimensions: 11.5 cm; 24 cm; 36.5 cm; 49 cm ... 99 cm etc.
External dimensions: 11.5 cm; 24 cm; 36.5 cm etc.
Aperture dimensions: 51 cm; 1.01 m; 1.26 m etc.
Projection dimensions: 12.5 cm; 25 cm; 1.00 m etc.

When bricks are cut, always remember to subtract a joint:

¾ brick = specified dimension/4 × 3 – joint = 6.25 cm × 3 – 1 cm
= 17.75 cm.

Cut units are specially designated in the top view on laying drawings: the ¾ unit (17.75 cm) by a diagonal, the ½ unit (11.5 cm) by a cross, and the ¼ unit (5.25 cm) by a point or a circle.

The octametric numerical values are used for height as well. To achieve the specified dimension height (25 cm, 50 cm, 1 m etc.), the horizontal mortar joints serve as a height levelling course, and thus measure between 1.05 and 1.22 cm.

BRICK COURSES

The individual rows in a masonry structure are called courses. A distinction is made according to the run of the bricks:

Stretcher course:	bricks are laid parallel with the axis of the wall
Header course:	bricks are laid transversely to the wall axis
Brick-on-edge course:	bricks are laid transversely and standing edgewise on their long sides
Soldier course:	bricks stand edgewise on their narrow sides as an upright header course

While the stretcher and header courses are combined with each other in different ways as bonds, the edge and soldier courses with their larger head joints offer greater bond strength between the bricks and better pressure dispersal, as they do not break as easily as a horizontal brick. They are therefore used for lintels, seatings and cornices.

MASONRY BONDS

To produce high-quality masonry with a good loadbearing capacity from bricks and mortar there are certain craft rules that must be followed when laying bricks – the bond rules. These rules distinguish between four so-called school bonds – those most commonly taught – according to the sequence in which the brick courses are laid on one another, and the way they are offset from each other.

Some of the bond rules are general, and give us the first two school bonds.

Rules:
_ All the courses must be laid horizontally.
_ The brick height should not be greater than the brick width.

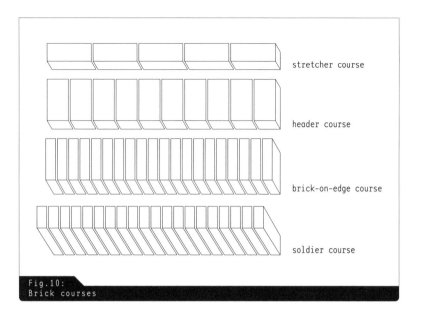

stretcher course

header course

brick-on-edge course

soldier course

Fig.10:
Brick courses

_ Only bricks of the same height should be used in a single course (only at wall ends can there be exceptions in every second course).
_ The largest possible number of whole bricks should be used.
_ The offset between the courses is at least ¼ brick length for all perpends.

The brick offset is crucial for the wall's loadbearing capacity. The greater the offset, i.e. the more shallow the racking back of the bricks, the greater the resistance to longitudinal cracks.

\\Hint:
The designation "brick length" also relates to the corresponding standard brick in terms of brick offsetting. But the joint must always be taken into account. Thus, with a specified dimension of 25 cm: ¼ brick length = specified dimension/4 - joint = 25 cm/4 - 1 cm = 5.25 cm. The same applies to the brick width or the wall thickness: a wall two bricks thick = 2 × 25 cm - 1 cm = 49 cm (external dimension).

19

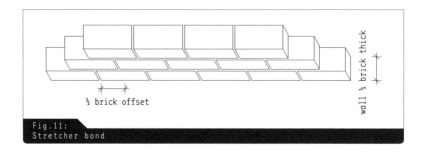

½ brick offset

wall ½ brick thick

Fig.11:
Stretcher bond

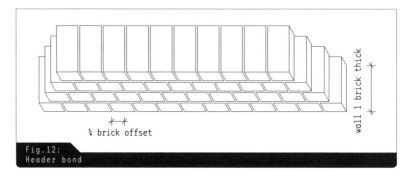

¼ brick offset

wall 1 brick thick

Fig.12:
Header bond

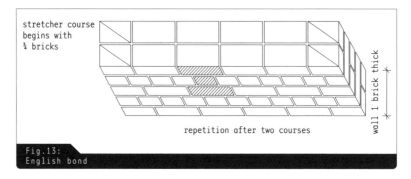

stretcher course
begins with
¾ bricks

repetition after two courses

wall 1 brick thick

Fig.13:
English bond

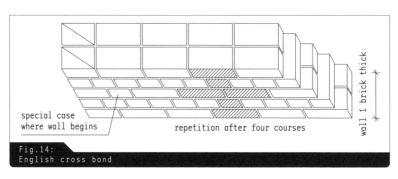

special case
where wall begins

repetition after four courses

wall 1 brick thick

Fig.14:
English cross bond

In stretcher bond, all courses in the masonry are made up of stretcher courses offset by the length of 1/2 brick. As this bond does not permit an offset running transversely to the wall axis, it can only be used for wall ½ brick thick, e.g. for internal walls, facer skins and chimneys. A wider wall can be built only with larger bricks. Stretcher bond offers good compressive and tensile strength because of the large brick offset. It is also possible to use an offset of ⅓ or ¼ of a brick length, but this entails some loss of loadbearing capacity.

In header bond, all the courses consist of header courses offset by the length of ¼ brick. This bond can only be used for one-brick walls. Because of the low overlap the bond has less loadbearing capacity and inclines to diagonal cracks because of the steep racking. It is however particularly suitable for narrow masonry radii.

Combining these bonds and following two more rules gives the last two commonly taught bonds.

Rules:
_ Stretcher and header courses alternate.
_ One stretcher course begins with a ¾ brick (for thicker walls, with correspondingly more ¾ bricks).

English bond consist of alternate courses of stretchers and headers. The offset is ¼ brick. This produces usefully shallow racking by ¼ and ¾ brick lengths in each case.

Like English bond, English cross bond begins with alternate stretcher and header courses. But the perpends of the stretcher courses are offset against each other by ½ brick, so the joint pattern repeats only every four courses. This bond has a more varied joint pattern, but it is also more steeply racked and therefore more prone to diagonal cracks.

There are also some decorative bonds, but these are only of historical or regional significance. Examples are double Flemish bond, Yorkshire bond and Flemish bond.

It is also possible to achieve a lateral offset within the wall, and so to construct walls with a thickness greater than one brick, by alternating stretcher and header courses.

Additional rules apply here:
_ Only headers should be used if possible for wide walls.

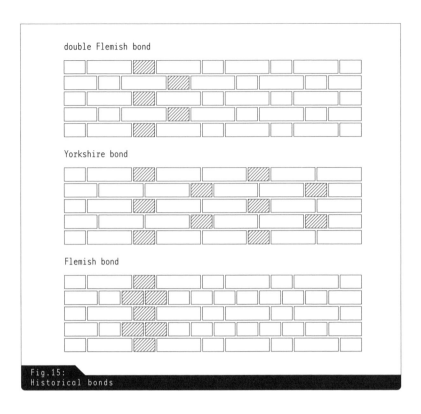

double Flemish bond

Yorkshire bond

Flemish bond

_ Perpends should run through the total thickness of the wall if possible.

_ The offset should also be at least ¼ brick length as the courses rise for the intermediate joints as well (perpends inside the wall).

_ The offset must be maintained longitudinally and horizontally.

REGULAR CONSTRUCTIONS

Corners in walls

For corners, niches, projections and columns, there are special points of detail covered by the bond rules.

Rules:

_ The stretcher courses run through at corners, junctions and joints; the header courses abut.

_ Parallel walls should have the same sequence of courses.

_ Only one perpend in each course should start from an inside corner.

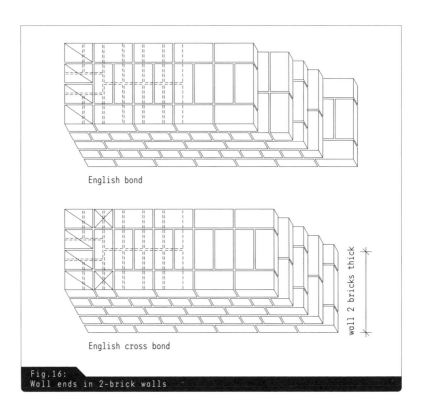

English bond

English cross bond

wall 2 bricks thick

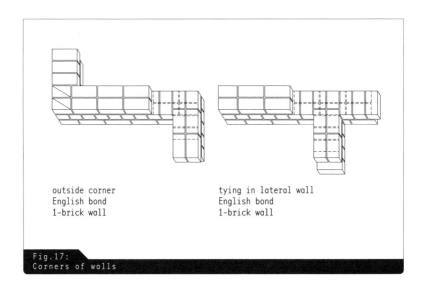

outside corner
English bond
1-brick wall

tying in lateral wall
English bond
1-brick wall

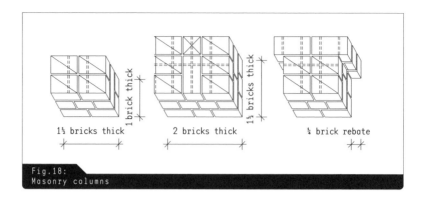

1½ bricks thick   2 bricks thick   ¼ brick rebate

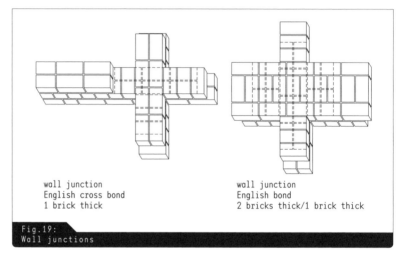

wall junction
English cross bond
1 brick thick

wall junction
English bond
2 bricks thick/1 brick thick

_ Windows and door strips should be constructed like wall ends with projections – for the headers by displacing one brick in the direction of the projection, for the stretchers by advancing the stretchers.

Masonry columns

Two points should be noted when constructing masonry columns:

_ Square columns have the same bond in every course, turned through 90° each time.
_ Rectangular columns start with ¾ bricks on the narrow sides, like wall ends. The gap is filled with whole or half bricks.

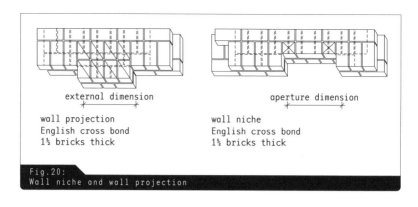

external dimension

wall projection
English cross bond
1½ bricks thick

aperture dimension

wall niche
English cross bond
1½ bricks thick

Fig.20:
Wall niche and wall projection

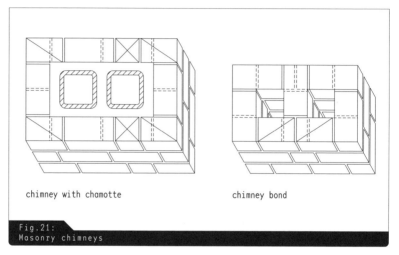

chimney with chamotte

chimney bond

Fig.21:
Masonry chimneys

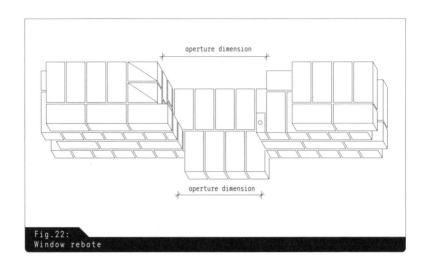

aperture dimension

aperture dimension

Fig.22:
Window rebate

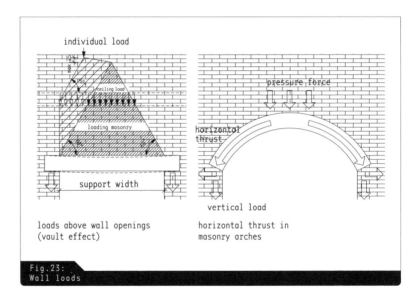

individual load

ceiling load

loading masonry

support width

loads above wall openings
(vault effect)

pressure force

horizontal thrust

vertical load

horizontal thrust in
masonry arches

Fig.23:
Wall loads

Masonry
apertures

Apertures for windows, doors or passageways in the wall are subject to craft rules and traditions, as well as the wall itself.

Side rebates for windows and doors can be constructed according to bonding rules; this simplifies installation and improves the fittings' resistance to rain and wind.

The top of the door or window can also be built according to the rules. As masonry cannot absorb bending forces, apertures cannot be topped with bonded masonry without "support", so beams, formerly made of wood or stone, and now of concrete, can be placed over the aperture. The beams dissipate the imposed load from the masonry above into the side walls through the structural conditions in terms of bending, restricting the possible size of the aperture according to the material used for the beam.

› 𝕀

Masonry arches Another aperture suitable for masonry is an arch with masonry above it, which transforms all the imposed loads into pressure forces and transfers them to their points of support. The difficulty of this construction lies in the horizontal thrust that the loaded arch exerts on the masonry. This thrust, which increases in shallower arches, must be absorbed either by the wall or by additional piers.

Round arches are semicircles of masonry that transfer the imposed load into support points, which are usually horizontal. The radius of the arch is thus half the width of the aperture and lies at its midpoint. To achieve this radius the joints between the bricks should be wedge-shaped. A thickness of at least 5 mm may be reached on the inside of the arch (intrados) and a maximum of 20 cm at the other extremity (extrados). This means that when dealing with larger radii and aperture widths, several rows of bricks must be placed on top of each other. Wedge-shaped bricks can also be used for tighter radii.

If the radius is increased to the full width of the aperture and circles are drawn around the two support points, a pointed arch is produced. Both types of arch should consist of an uneven number of bricks, so that a keystone, which starts the load distribution, can be placed at the apex of the arch, rather than a perpend. The keystone should end in a bed joint of the masonry, so that the filler courses above the apex of the arch do not

𝕀
\\ Hint:
Because of the so-called "vault effect" of the masonry, which transfers the loads around the aperture, only the self-weight of the masonry above the apertures affects the beam, relating to a triangular load take-up area. In addition there are single loads, provided that they are not more than 25 cm above the tip of the take-up areas, and ceiling loads, if they are within the take-up area (see Fig. 23).

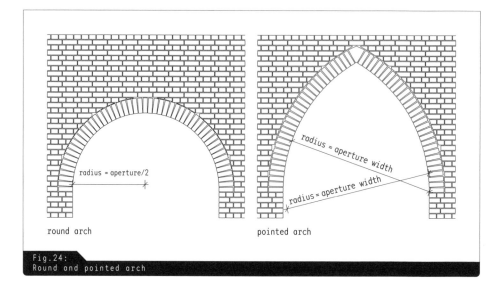

radius = aperture/2

round arch

radius = aperture width
radius = aperture width

pointed arch

Fig.24:
Round and pointed arch

become too large. For window rebates, arches can be built in two rows of bricks, displaced vertically.

If the surrounding loadbearing structure is able to absorb greater horizontal forces, a shallower arch structure may be chosen. For a segmental arch a circular sector with a greater radius is built; here the rise of the arch (the difference in height between the lowest and the highest point of the inside of the arch) must not be greater than 1/12 of the aperture width. The support points are tilted to point towards the centre of the arch.

If the aperture is built over almost horizontally as a result of the sideways tilt of the bricks, the term "straight arch" is used. Here the rise is reduced to a maximum of 1/50 of the aperture width.

The aperture width is strictly limited for both these construction methods. The following formula can be used as a rule of thumb:

_ 1.2 m for segmental arch with bricks 24 cm high
_ 0.8 m for straight arch with bricks 25 cm high

Masonry arches are very elaborate structures, commonly associated with churches and prestigious buildings, and are now only rarely built. Today the arches can be manufactured with steel reinforcements and built in as finished parts.

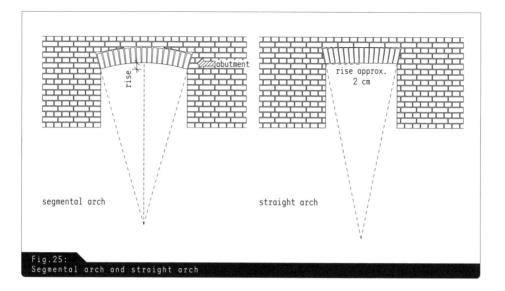

segmental arch   straight arch

rise

abutment

rise approx.
2 cm

Fig.25:
Segmental arch and straight arch

JOINT CONFIGURATIONS

In addition to masonry bonds, the configuration of the mortar joints can make a considerable contribution to the appearance of the masonry. The colour or depth of the joints can emphasize them or make them inconspicuous for design purposes.

Executing joints correctly also makes the structure more resistant, and helps it to last longer. There are two kinds of joint:

Flush pointing

For trowel-finished joints the mortar pushed out at the sides when a brick is put in place is struck off and smoothed down a little later with a piece of wood or a hose. The advantage of this method lies in the good seal it creates for the joint and the need to apply the mortar to the whole surface, which improves the loadbearing capacity of the masonry.

\\ Example:
Frank Lloyd Wright emphasized the horizontal orientation of his Robie House in Chicago by recessing the bed joints and using flush perpends.

Fig.26:
Joints

Subsequent
pointing
However, if the uniformity of the joints is important in terms of colour and design, it can be advantageous to point subsequently. Here, the fresh mortar is scratched out with a wooden lath to a depth of about 20 mm and the opening cleaned; if absorbent bricks, which draw the water out of the mortar, are being used, the opening must be moistened before being closed again with the pointing mortar. Attention must be paid to high-quality finish because of the two kinds of mortar; this will guarantee the loadbearing capacity and density of the construction.

FINISHING RULES

Masonry must be bonded, and also built horizontal, true and plumb. The first course is crucial, as it compensates for uneven terrain. The rows of bricks should then be laid from the corners. This can be done by hand up to a weight of 25 kg per brick, above which auxiliary equipment is needed. The mortar must be applied to the full area of the bed joints; for small bricks with a trowel, for larger sizes with a mortar template, which keeps the height of the joints consistent over the full length of the wall. The perpends must also be closed to ensure that the masonry is rain- and wind-proof, either by covering the full surface with mortar or by flushing mortar pockets in the middle of the brick. To save time and expense, masonry is sometimes built without using mortar for the perpends. But here it is essential to meet all the demands of weather protection (by using a layer of rendering or cladding) and sound insulation (good sound-reducing bricks). Bricks using a tongue and groove system are preferred for this.

If highly absorbent bricks are being used, care should be taken before laying them to dampen the wall, as the bricks will draw too much water out of the drying mortar. The bricks will then also absorb fewer salts from the mortar that would later be visible on the surface of the brick as

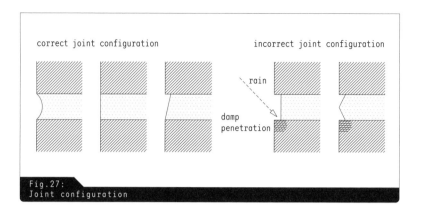

"efflorescence". At the same time, a completely soaked brick will prevent proper binding with the mortar. Bricks and masonry should therefore be protected against rain, as well as against unduly strong sunlight. In frost, bricks can only be laid if precautions are taken, as mortar hardens more slowly with falling temperatures, and stops hardening altogether at –10 °C. Building materials should be covered as soon as the temperature falls to 5 °C, and at temperatures under 0 °C bricks and mixing water should be warmed. Frozen materials should not be used, and parts of the wall that have already been damaged must be removed.

BUILDING IN STONE

Natural stone is the Ur-form of masonry. From the simple, mortarless piling up of unworked stones in various sizes (drystone walling) to stones of equal sizes laid according to bonding rules (ashlar masonry), there are various special types of natural stone masonry. However, natural stones are now used less for actual masonry than as curtain façade material for

ρ

\\ Example:
Arno Lederer chose this colour design option for his office building in Stuttgart. He used a black brick and pointed the perpends in black as well, but the bed joints are white. This gives the façade an unmistakable appearance (see Fig. 26, second picture from the left).

walls, and therefore they will not be dealt with more fully here. Exceptions
are primarily found in monument protection and landscape architecture.

NEW APPROACHES

In addition to the traditional building method prescribed by the
bonding rules, new approaches have developed, based on new manufacturing methods and building materials, intended above all to make masonry
construction cheaper and less time-consuming.

Moulded brick masonry

For moulded brick masonry, the dimension tolerance of the bricks
has been minimized so that the joint height can be reduced to 1–3 mm
(thin bed). The mortar is applied with a roller, or the bricks are dipped in
the water. As the joint proportion is minimized and homogeneous masonry
produced, material and time are saved, and favourable statical values
achieved, › see chapter Masonry structures, Structural behaviour and there are fewer
thermal bridges.

› 🔟

As the brick rows can only accommodate low tolerances, the first
layer should be laid with great care. Small offset blocks can be used for
this purpose. They are available in different heights and with good insulation properties.

Dry masonry

Dry masonry uses no mortar at all. For reasons of loadbearing capacity, however, such wall constructions are restricted to low storey and
building heights. The ceiling loads on the walls must be even, so that this
pressure can compensate for the lack of adhesion from the mortar.

Masonry kits

To save the time needed for cutting large stones to size, masonry
kits offer the possibility of assembling whole sections of walls in the right

32

dimensions in the factory, and delivering them to the site as individual parts with a laying plan. This method is a reasonably priced alternative, particularly if there are many diagonals (gable walls) or apertures.

Prefabrication construction method   This method takes prefabrication a little further at the factory stage: manufacturers deliver whole storey-height walls, including apertures, to the site. The bricks have to be reinforced to stabilize the structure and erection requires a crane or mobile crane. The expense is set off against the consistent quality of the factory work (although the erector is of course responsible for the wall connection points).

MASONRY STRUCTURES

The structures listed below refer to the wall in its built state. The construction rules explained above apply in principle to all masonry structures, and deal merely with assembling bricks and mortar. There are various ways of finishing a construction, combinations with other building materials and dependencies on other parts of a building. These relate to the location where the building is to be used and the role of the wall structures.

Masonry walls can be loaded vertically from ceilings and other parts of the building, by self-weight and also by horizontal forces such as wind, soil pressure and impact forces, or cantilever loads from projecting or suspended elements.

For these reasons the walls must be connected non-positively with the adjacent building parts, i.e. the loads must be transferred via other loadbearing sections or directly into the foundations. The wall is stabilized by tie walls that prevent buckling, and by even vertical loading. When dimensioning these walls, there are more requirements relating to the building science of fire protection to meet. Walls supporting nothing more than their own weight from one floor and forces occurring horizontally to the wall level can also be built as non-loadbearing.

STRUCTURAL BEHAVIOUR

The loadbearing capacity of masonry is determined by the bonding of brick and mortar. The adhesion or friction between brick and mortar affect how horizontal forces are absorbed and provide vertical load distribution over the full area; the joint compensates for brick tolerances. Its ability to absorb compressive forces is far greater than its acceptance of tensile or tensile bending forces, i.e. a precisely bedded brick can transfer loads as compressive force but would break without this bedding surface. The brick and its mortar joint are pressed together from above in vertical loading. The brick conducts the compressive forces, and the mortar, which is more easily deformed, tries to sag. These different behaviours produce stress at the point of contact between bricks and mortar, and then to compressive stress in the mortar and tensile stress in the brick. At the same time, this lateral tensile stress in the brick reduces its compressive strength. If the load becomes too great, vertical cracks will appear in the brick and the mortar will collapse. Uneven application of mortar increases tension peaks and the danger of collapse. Greater join thicknesses and the use of

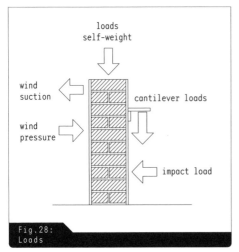

Fig.28:
Loads

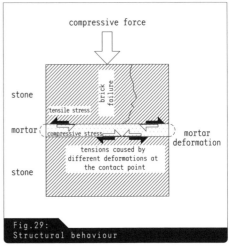

Fig.29:
Structural behaviour

lightweight mortar are also hazardous because of their greater deform-ability. Heavy bricks with a high specific density transfer forces well.

Aerated bricks and cavities weaken the cross-section and thus load-bearing capacity. Adhesion between bricks and mortar also allows force to be absorbed horizontally.

The brick's compressive strength is another crucial factor. Brick and mortar must also be matched to each other to avoid the joint collapsing. Compressive strength classes are given as characteristic values for both bricks and mortar.

EXTERNAL WALLS

External masonry walls are loadbearing walls, except for infill within other loadbearing systems (frame construction, construction slabs

> \\ Hint:
> Specific density is the ratio of mass to volume. As it is increased by absorbing water, this value is usually given for dry bricks, the dry density, in kg/m³.

etc.), or free-standing walls. They also separate the inside of the building from the outside, and so must give protection against cold, rain, snow and sound from the outside. At the same time, design questions play a part in decisions about whether the masonry should be visible from the outside or not.

Single-leaf
masonry External walls with just one wall built in bond are called single-leaf masonry. This structure, simple to erect in terms of craftsmanship, has to perform all the functions of an outside wall.

Single-leaf
exposed masonry Single-leaf exposed masonry, a wall structure that is visible from both sides or at least from the outside, displays a disparity between thermal insulation and weather protection. In order to meet today's thermal insulation criteria, aerated bricks providing offering good insulation must be used. As still air has a very low capacity for specific thermal heat conductivity and very low density, bricks with a high proportion of air in the form of pores or cavities, and thus a low specific density, provide good thermal insulation, but at the same time scarcely any protection against weather.

> 🔊

Their pores quickly become permeated with moisture, they are not frost-resistant and thus not suitable for unprotected use. Conversely, weather-resistant bricks with a high specific density offer little resistance to heat penetration and would require uneconomic wall thicknesses. This structure can therefore no longer be used in this way.

> 🔊

Facing masonry For facing masonry, on the other hand, a wall several units thick between two different kinds of masonry is used inside the bond, so that the bricks showing on the outside offer good protection against weather and frost, and the inner series takes over the thermal insulation. Here the whole cross-section including the facing can be added to the load dispersal;

🔊

\\ Hint:
The specific thermal conductivity (λ) indicates how much heat a structural element will transfer under fixed conditions. The smaller the value, the better the thermal insulation.

🔊

\\ Hint:
The thermal transfer resistance (R) indicates a structural element's insulation capacity, according to its thickness. It is calculated from the ratio of course thickness to specific heat conductivity. The transitions at the extremities of the element are also calculated, and the individual values added for multi-course elements.

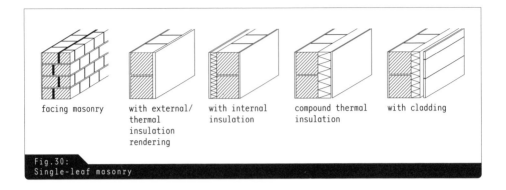

facing masonry | with external/ thermal insulation rendering | with internal insulation | compound thermal insulation | with cladding

Fig.30:
Single-leaf masonry

the brick with the lowest compressive strength provides the basis for calculations. A joint between the two series of stones, offset course-wise, 2 cm thick and closed with seal mortar, offers protection for the inner set of units. This is an elaborate structure, and the units in it must be well matched to each other, in order to avoid different settling rates and deformations. Very precise planning is also needed, because unit formats often differ. This structure is recommended only for visual or formal reasons, or if a special brick is to be used or there is a request to manage without expansion joints in the exposed masonry. ˃ see chapter External walls

Because of all these interdependent features, additional measures have to be taken with single-leaf masonry to protect it from the weather.

Single-leaf masonry with external rendering

Thus, for example, external rendering can be applied; this improves thermal insulation as thermal insulation rendering. The visual effect of bonded masonry is lost in single-leaf masonry with external rendering, but large-format units can be used, built in random bond with a thin mortar bed. They have better insulation properties, and are economical to use. As the whole cross-section of the wall contributes to the thermal insulation, weaknesses must be avoided to prevent thermal bridges. Special constructions are needed, especially for lintels and ceiling supports.

Ceiling supports

˃ 𝟘

Ceilings must be connected with the enclosing walls by their supports on the wall via adhesions and friction. As a rule a bearing edge of 10–12 cm is needed.

˃ 𝒫

As reinforced concrete has a lower heat transfer resistance than masonry, full support for the ceiling reduces thermal insulation. This produces colder ceiling and wall areas, and moisture from warm interior air may condense on their inside faces.

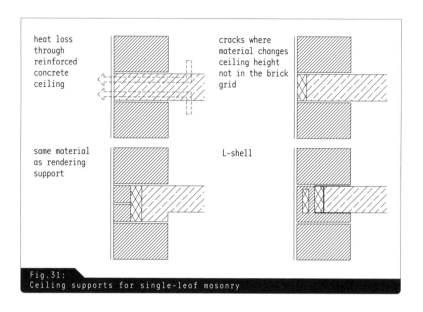

heat loss through reinforced concrete ceiling

cracks where material changes ceiling height not in the brick grid

same material as rendering support

L-shell

Fig.31:
Ceiling supports for single-leaf masonry

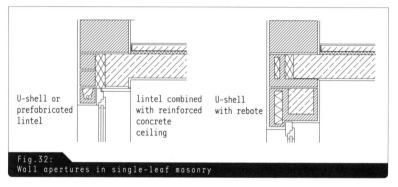

U-shell or prefabricated lintel

lintel combined with reinforced concrete ceiling

U-shell with rebate

Fig.32:
Wall apertures in single-leaf masonry

\\ Hint:
If there is not enough area to support the ceiling, steel tie bars must be fixed into the masonry. As this exposes the masonry to horizontal tensile forces, the wall areas must receive a corresponding imposed load to counter the tensile forces. This means that ties cannot be fixed in parapet areas. Gable walls can also be attached to the roof structure with tie bars.

\\ Example:
Condensate: Warm air can hold more water vapour than cold air. If warm air meets cold air, mist or water vapour is formed. If warm air meets a cold object, excess water is released, forming a condensate. For heated air in a room, if an outside wall is poorly insulated, or even not insulated at all, water will be deposited on the cold internal side or in the cooled structural element. This then leads to structural damage from frost or mould.

For this reason, additional insulation must be provided at the outer edge of the ceiling. It should be noted here that single-leaf rendered walls may be subject to cracks on the outside because of different expansion and deformation at the point where the different materials meet, so that rain may penetrate the building. Fabric can be applied to bridge the point of transition and secure the rendering, but the use of L-shells is also recommended. These are made of the same material as the wall, and some already have insulation strips. They avoid the change of material while acting as a formwork element for the reinforced concrete.

> 🛈

Wall apertures

These weaknesses also occur for wall apertures. As masonry cannot accept tensile or bending loads, it is impossible to build across a wall aperture without support. Additional beams are needed to resist the loads and transfer them transversely into the adjacent parts of the wall. As steel does not meet fire protection criteria, these beams are usually made of reinforced concrete and, like the ceilings, must have additional thermal insulation or be built using U-shells. These special parts can either be made on the spot, e.g. at the same time as the concrete ceiling is cast, or delivered to the site as prefabricated lintels, reinforced in the factory.

Tie bars / ring beams

U-shells can also be used to create peripheral tie beams and ring beams. Other factors, such as wind forces, cause tensile forces in a building. These are transferred by the ceilings as sheets and cannot be absorbed by the walls alone. Peripheral tie beams can be made in the form of reinforced concrete beams or U-shells under the ceiling, or of appropriately reinforced ceiling strips. They transfer forces for all external and transverse walls. In the case of ceilings with no sheet action or with sliding supports (e.g. under flat roofs) the peripheral tie beams should run round the whole building as a continuous ring (ring beam).

🛈

\\Hint:
L- or U-shells are available from brick manufacturers as prefabricated parts. As the name suggests, the L-shell is L-shaped, to support the ceiling. U-shells are used above wall apertures and to create ring beams. The cavity is filled with concrete on site (see Fig. 31).

To improve the wall structure's thermal insulation properties, insulation or thermal insulation rendering can be applied to its internal side. This construction is problematical in terms of building science, however, as there is a danger that condensate will form on the inside of the cold masonry and impregnate the construction with moisture, which may lead to mould formation. For this reason, this method tends to be used for refurbishment, when it is not permissible to alter listed façades.

To avoid these problems, the insulation is not fixed inside in a laminated thermal insulation system, but stuck onto the masonry and fixed with ties. To protect the insulation from the weather, however, a special layer of water- or moisture-resistant rendering is applied directly to the insulating material. As the rendering needs a solid ground, and as no holes or pressure points should be created by external factors, the insulation must resist compression and provide sufficient general resistance. LHIS is a common system for reasons of economy, above all when refurbishing existing buildings.

Another way of protecting loadbearing masonry is to suspend an outer skin in front of the building. This structure made of metal, wood or fibre cement can be attached directly to the masonry, or a space can be left for an additional insulating layer. Care should be taken with the fixing points, which could cool the masonry, and adequate rear ventilation to prevent moisture impregnation from water that gets behind the cladding.

Basement walls are single-leaf in all structures. An approach using waterproof reinforced concrete ("White Tub") is increasingly common, but another wall structure may be preferable. Basement walls need to be well reinforced against soil pressure, which affects the surface of the wall vertically, and against load transfer. When fixing dimensions, wall height, soil pressure and the superimposed load from the surface of the terrain should be taken into account. The thermal insulation that is applied outside (perimeter insulation) also has to be able to stand up to the soil pressure in working basement spaces with high thermal insulation demands, and must therefore be compression resistant. It can be made of sheet foamed glass, polystyrene particle foam or extruded polystyrene foam sheets. Basement walls must also be sealed against moisture in the soil. A concrete finish is preferred if there is heavy potential pressure from water, but if the load is less and the water does not exert pressure, horizontal and vertical sealing should be provided. The horizontal membrane in the form of a sealing sheet should be applied to the full area of the concrete slab, and must join up with vertical sealing in the form of

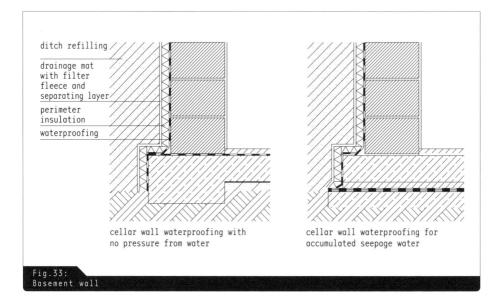

ditch refilling

drainage mat
with filter
fleece and
separating layer

perimeter
insulation

waterproofing

cellar wall waterproofing with
no pressure from water

cellar wall waterproofing for
accumulated seepage water

Fig.33:
Basement wall

sheets or bituminous coatings on the on the outside of the wall under the first row of bricks. Finish as a "Black Tub" provides additional protection: here the horizontal membrane is attached onto a base course under the floor slab and given a protective coating. Both the vertical membrane and any possible thermal insulation can be protected against soil damage when the excavation pit is filled, by using a protective layer of geotextile membrane and filter fleece, which also drains off water.

Plinth zone

The plinth zone is more heavily loaded than the masonry above it by the adjacent soil and the effects of splash water. Hence, it should be sealed against moisture by a vertical membrane to a height of 30 cm above the top edge of the terrain. This ends with a horizontal damp course the full width of the wall, which prevents moisture from rising further into the masonry above it. This damp course should be protected by a row of weatherproof bricks, by cladding, or by applying a special water-resistant plinth rendering. The transition between the renderings can be carried out through the structure or by using differences in smoothness. Plaster bases, e.g. in expanded metal, help to avoid cracks at this point.

Double-leaf
masonry

In double-leaf masonry, a second wall (external or facing leaf), which protects the inner side from the weather, is built in front of an inner wall (inner leaf), which has the primary loadbearing function. A gap is left

42

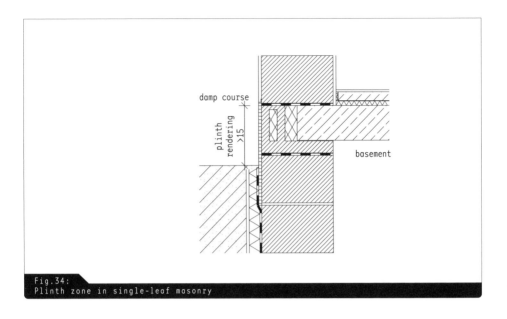

damp course

plinth
rendering
>15

basement

Fig.34:
Plinth zone in single-leaf masonry

between them (cavity), which can be left free, or wholly or partially filled with insulation.

Double-leaf masonry with cavity

The cavity is there to prevent water penetrating directly into the inner leaf and thus into the interior, and causing damage such as mould formation. If moisture has penetrated the outer leaf, it is removed via the cavity. To this end, ventilation apertures should be placed in the plinth area and at the top of the wall and wall apertures. These are usually open perpends with a horizontal damp course. This is achieved by laying a sealant strip or film as a "Z-barrier" across the full area of the bed joint below the open settlement joints, and taking it to the inner leaf with an incline of 1–2 cm and then 15 cm upwards.

\\ Important:
For all sealing membranes, special attention should be paid to points at which a wall or ceiling is penetrated by sanitation pipes or service connections, which must be carefully sealed.

with cavity

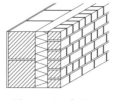
with core insulation

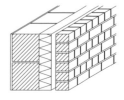
with insulation and cavity

Fig.35:
Double-leaf masonry

To ensure adequate back ventilation, the air gap should be at least 60 mm wide, or 40 mm if the joint mortar is cleaned off or if insulation is used. Although vertical air gaps – including the back ventilation – conduct little heat, for thermal insulation it is usually necessary to fit an insulating layer in the gap. If the entire gap between the leaves is filled, this is called double-leaf masonry with core insulation.

Full-fill cavity walls

This version increases the resistance to heat transfer, but not the thickness of the brick, and thus the thickness of the whole wall. The insulation can be in the form of blankets or strips fastened to the inner leaf, or loose granules or mixtures, which are shaken into the gap; care must be taken to distribute them evenly. The disadvantage of this structure lies in the fact that water can get in behind the front leaf. It is difficult to remove, and reduces the thermal insulation properties of the structure, as damp building materials transfer heat better than dry ones. The insulation material must therefore be permanently water-resistant, and joints and connection points must prevent water from penetrating. Softer mineral fibre strips should be packed tightly, and plastic foams given a stepped rebate or tongue and groove. Any damage caused by fixing the blankets or the outer leaf should be sealed. If insulation material is poured or shaken in, care should be taken that no material can fall out of the drainage apertures, e.g. by installing a rustproof perforated grille.

Double-leaf masonry with insulation and air gap combines the advantages of the two above-mentioned constructions.

44

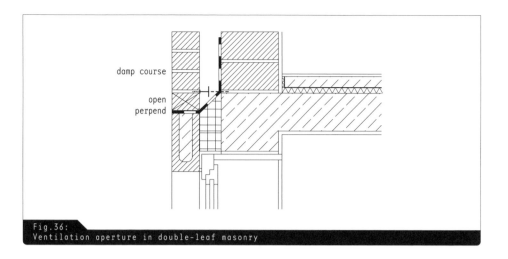

damp course

open
perpend

Fig.36:
Ventilation aperture in double-leaf masonry

Partial-fill
cavity walls

A layer of water-resistant thermal-insulation blankets or mats is at-tached to the inner leaf and separated from the outer leaf by an air gap of at least 4 cm. This is more elaborate to build than other constructions. As loadbearing, insulation, damp and weather protection are strictly separated, it offers the best properties, but the whole structure will be thicker.

Inner leaf

In all constructions, the inner leaf serves mainly to provide struc-tural stability and transfer load. It can be built with loadbearing bricks of a high specific density; these have low resistance to heat transfer, but offer a high level of sound insulation. Essentially, all standard bricks and mortars approved by the building authorities can be used for the inner leaf. › see chapter Building materials As the inner side usually has a layer of internal rendering applied to it that covers the bricks, large blocks can be used, running counter to the bonding rules, as they are built in random bond and with a thin mortar bed, but are very strong. Supporting concrete ceilings is not a problem for insulated versions. Thermal insulation can be placed continuously in front of the inner leaf. The full area of the ceiling can be supported by it and thermal insulation can be additionally improved where appropriate by placing an insulating strip in front of it.

External leaf

The external leaf protects the rest of the masonry from external fac-tors and the weather. For this reason, only materials should be used that are appropriate for these conditions and are not sensitive to frost, mois-ture and the effects of being on the outside. Such units are offered by brick,

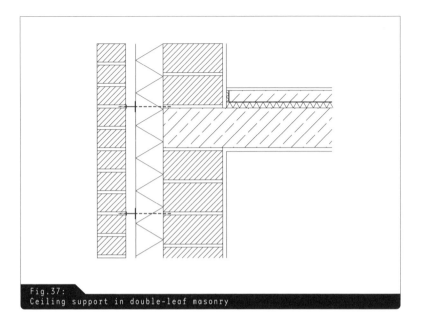

Fig.37:
Ceiling support in double-leaf masonry

calcium silicate and concrete block manufacturers as frost-proof, facing or vitrified units. › see chapter Building materials Mortar manufacturers also offer special frost-resistant mortars that absorb little water and are low in efflorescence, i.e. do not discolour as a result of salt deposits.

The outer leaf determines the appearance of the building and is ideally built in the commonly taught bonds described above. But this leaf can absorb only its own self-weight and has to be fixed to the inner leaf by wire anchors to secure it against wind pressure or suction, and avoid tipping over, collapsing or bulging. The number of anchors needed and their diameter depend on the distance between the leaves and the height of the wall. Separate attention should be paid to open edges of apertures, corners of the building or expansion joints, as well as rounded parts of the structure. The appropriate measures must be taken to prevent moisture from being transported from the outer to the inner leaf, such as fitting plastic discs so that the water can drip off in the gap.

Underpinning   In addition to wall-anchor fixing, the outer leaf must be regularly underpinned and attached to the inner leaf, so that at greater heights the self-weight can be transferred evenly into the loadbearing leaf, as well as being supported by the base. Rustproof bracket anchors and angle-brackets or thermally isolated ceiling projections are used for this.

46

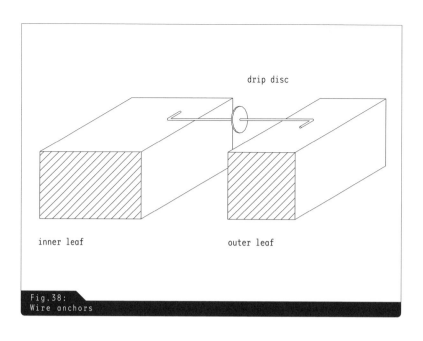

Fig.38:
Wire anchors

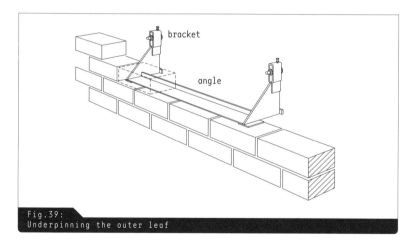

Fig.39:
Underpinning the outer leaf

The leaf must be secured against slipping away at the base. The first run of anchors should therefore be placed as low as possible. The lower sealing strip should extend to the front edge of the outer leaf.

The minimum thickness for the outer leaf is 9 cm. Anything thinner is referred to as wall cladding. > see chapter External walls For reasons of space

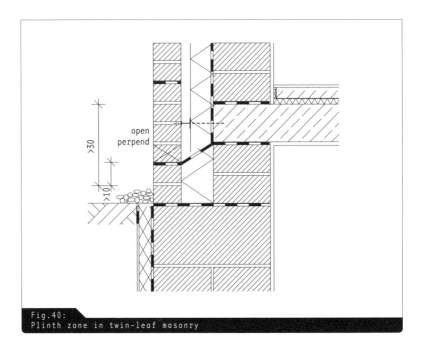

open
perpend

Fig.40:
Plinth zone in twin-leaf masonry

and thus of expense, the outer leaf is usually half a brick thick, so the visible bonds are not regular, as the most commonly taught bonds (except the stretcher bond) cannot be built in this way.

Apertures

For aesthetic reasons, the bond should generally run throughout the area of the wall. Apertures, windows and doors and any projections therefore need special anchors to hold the units in position. Lintels are often built in soldier bond, which is however not a regular construction, unlike the arch constructions described above, and cannot carry any load. The bricks should therefore be supported by brackets, which is cheap, but visible from the outside. Or there may be an invisible joint reinforcement to hold the bricks in place. Brick manufacturers also offer U-shells, which are reinforced and filled with concrete. These constructions transfer the load into the wall areas adjacent at the sides. All metal parts should be rustproof, ideally made of stainless steel, as galvanized items can be damaged in transport or fitting, and flaws are hard to see or reach after fitting.

Joints

The outer leaf deforms differently from the inner leaf as a result of temperature and weather. Vertical and horizontal movement joints should

48

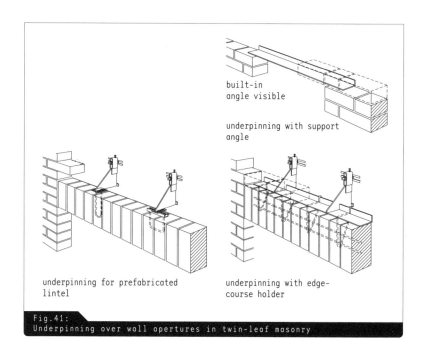

built-in
angle visible

underpinning with support
angle

underpinning for prefabricated
lintel

underpinning with edge-
course holder

Fig.41:
Underpinning over wall apertures in twin-leaf masonry

therefore be planned for the outer leaf to absorb this deformation. As well as the material-dependent distances between the expansion joints, › see Table 1 the walls should be separated at the corners on the basis of factors relating to the points of the compass. The west wall expands most, and the north wall least. These joints can however be offset by half the gap between the joints towards the middle, if this is architecturally desirable. Cracks around window sills caused by different loading of sill and the masonry around it can also be prevented by expansion joints on both sides. Structural reinforcement in the upper sill area may replace these joints. Horizontal joints should always be planned under the underpinning.

Non-loadbearing external walls – free-standing walls

Free-standing walls are very restricted in terms of height, as they are supported only at the base point and have no stabilizing imposed load. The walls must therefore be thicker or stabilized by crosswalls or columns. As they are outdoors and exposed to frost, they must use frost-resistant materials and foundations and be protected against moisture. Horizontal dampproof courses are needed above ground level, and the top of the wall should be protected by blocks, metal sheeting or concrete coping and damp courses.

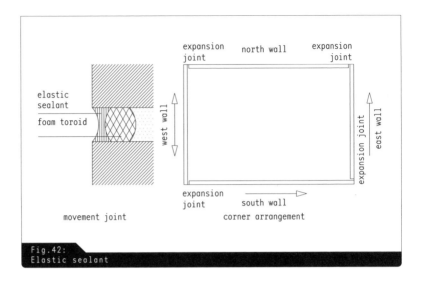

Fig.42:
Elastic sealant

Image labels: expansion joint, north wall, expansion joint, elastic sealant, foam toroid, west wall, expansion joint, east wall, expansion joint, south wall, movement joint, corner arrangement

Table 1:
Distance between joints

Masonry in	Distance between the expansion joints in m
calcium silicate brick, aerated concrete block, concrete block	6–8
lightweight concrete block	4–6
brick	10–20

From: P. Schubert: Zweischalige Aussenwände – Dehnungsfugen in der Aussenschale (Verblendschale), in: Mauerwerk 6/2003, Ernst & Sohn, Berlin, p.203

Figure 44 shows a comparison between different wall structures using the same brick. The lower the given thermal transfer coefficient U, the better the thermal insulation. The relationship of the results is more important than the precise value.

INTERNAL WALLS

Internal walls are not directly connected to the outdoors. They are already protected from cold, rain and snow by the external walls, ceilings and floors. Their main function is to separate internal areas, use zones or sightlines. The separation may require greater sound insulation, e.g. between dwellings, between bedrooms and living areas, between office and production areas, or it may have a fire protection function.

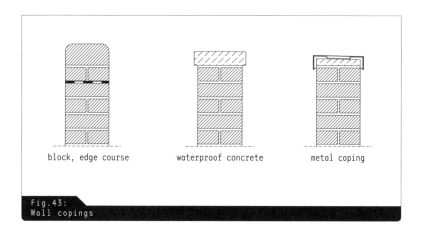

block, edge course   waterproof concrete   metal coping

Fig.43:
Wall copings

Some inner walls also have to carry part of the load of the building, or stiffen the building or individual sections of wall. They can thus be loadbearing in direct connection with the adjacent structural elements, or non-loadbearing, in which case all they have to do to avoid falling over is transfer their self-weight and the horizontal loads on their area to other structural elements. These different requirements are reflected in both the dimensioning and the detail of the connection points. Specific density affects compressive strength and above all sound insulation, and plays a key part in relation to internal walls. Here, units with a high mass and specific density offer both great compressive strength and good sound insulation.

Loadbearing and stiffening internal walls Loadbearing internal walls stiffen the building and provide ceiling supports. To stiffen a wall, the connection with it should be tension- and compression-resistant; building materials with approximately the same deformation behaviour should be chosen where possible for the sake of stability. Connection is achieved by building both walls to the same height in bond or by leaving gaps (socket connection) or protruding bricks (projection connection) in the wall to be stiffened, which will be worked on

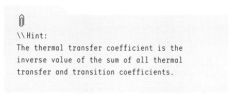

\\ Hint:
The thermal transfer coefficient is the inverse value of the sum of all thermal transfer and transition coefficients.

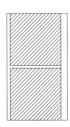
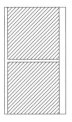
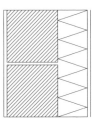

with external
rendering

with thermal insulation
rendering

compound thermal
insulation system

light mineral rendering
2 cm 0.31 W/mK
transverse brick 30 cm 0.14 W/mK
internal rendering 1.5 cm 0.7 W/mK

U=0.417 W/m²K

thermal insulation rendering
3 cm 0.07 W/mK
transverse brick 30 cm 0.14 W/mK
internal rendering 1.5 cm 0.7 W/mK

U=0.362 W/m²K

compound thermal insulation
system 6 cm 0.035 W/mK
transverse brick 30 cm 0.14 W/mK
internal rendering 1.5 cm 0.7 W/mK

U=0.234 W/m²K

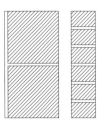
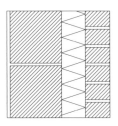
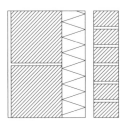

with cavity

with core insulation

with insulation and cavity

facing 11.5 cm 0.68 W/mK
cavity, wire anchors 4 cm
transverse brick 30 cm 0.14 W/mK
internal rendering 1.5 cm 0.7 W/mK

U=0.412 W/m²K

facing 11.5 cm 0.68 W/mK
core insulation 6 cm 0.35 W/mK
transverse brick 30 cm 0.14 W/mK
internal rendering 1.5 cm 0.7 W/mK

U=0.236 W/m²K

facing 11.5 cm 0.68 W/mK
cavity (wire anchors) 4 cm
core insulation 6 cm 0.035 W/mK
transverse brick 30 cm 0.14 W/mK
internal rendering 1.5 cm 0.7 W/mK

U=0.242 W/m²K

Fig.44:
Comparison of wall construction types

subsequently. The stiffening wall can thus be erected later, an advantage if additional space is needed, e.g. for scaffolding. However, this method does require additional reinforcing bars in the joints to absorb the tensile forces.

An efficient alternative is butt walling, which also requires tensile bars or anchors; the joint is pointed subsequently. This connection can be used only at internal corners, and has the advantage that when connecting with the external walls the thermal insulation of the external wall is not compromised by the intrusion of interlocking bricks from the internal wall, which could be made of different materials.

Party walls

Walls separating adjacent dwellings must always be twin-leaf structures for sound insulation purposes. The cavity width depends on the mass of the partitioning leaves; a width of 5 cm is recommended. The cavity should be filled with tightly packed mineral fibre blankets covering the full surface. Sound insulation is improved further by lagging in two layers with offset seams. Rigid foam sheets are inadmissible. Care should always be taken that no mortar drops into the joint. When building or attaching ceilings, the insulation should always be continued above the edge of the wall or ceiling.

Non-loadbearing
internal walls

Non-loadbearing internal walls may not be used for either stiffening or load transfer, and must not be subjected to wind loads. They carry all their self-weight and light bracket loads (e.g. shelves, pictures etc.), and must transfer impact loads to adjacent structural elements. Wall lengths have been calculated according to height, the way in which the wall is attached to adjacent structural elements (two-sided to four-sided mounting), and possible imposed loads from ceiling deformations. They are presented in a table that may be used without acknowledgement.

> ♀

Connections to adjacent structural elements can be rigid or sliding. Rigid connections should be used when there is little load from other structural elements that could lead to indirect stresses. They have good sound insulation and fire protection properties, and are inconspicuous as they are carried out without mortaring, steel inlays or interlocking.

Sliding connections are made using steel sections or sliding joint anchors and can absorb some deformations. These connections are very elaborate and may be visible, or need to be covered.

♀
\\ Important:
Special calculations must be applied to
masonry with unpointed perpends!

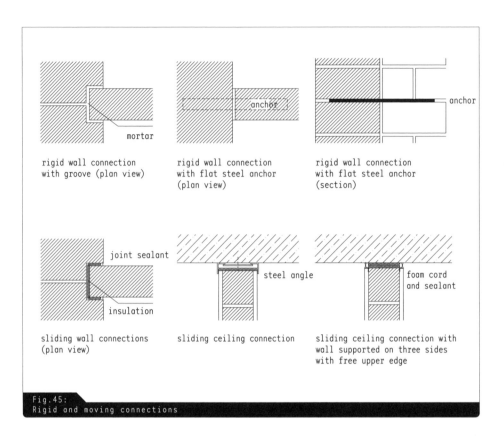

rigid wall connection
with groove (plan view)

rigid wall connection
with flat steel anchor
(plan view)

rigid wall connection
with flat steel anchor
(section)

sliding wall connections
(plan view)

sliding ceiling connection

sliding ceiling connection with
wall supported on three sides
with free upper edge

Fig.45:
Rigid and moving connections

SLOTS AND GAPS

When dimensioning walls, care should be taken when compromising the cross-section with slots and holes, e.g. for electrical or sanitary installations. Limiting values must not be exceeded. Many manufacturers offer special masonry units that already provide apertures for installations.

Earlier chapters describe masonry units in general terms and distinguish them only in terms of dimensions, geometry or the place where they are to be used. The question now arises of which material is suitable for a particular construction and the functions it has to perform. Various kinds of brick and mortar are listed and distinguished below.

MASONRY UNIT TYPES

In addition to the many types of natural stone, which will not be considered in detail here because they are so seldom used as pure masonry units in building construction, there is an equally wide variety of artificially manufactured bricks and blocks. To fulfil the functions of masonry – supporting, separating, facing, insulating, protecting – they are finished in a variety of ways, and have many different properties. The following summary can be made on the basis of the above-mentioned relationship between the unit's specific density and the requirements:

high dry specific density	=	good compressive strength
high dry specific density	=	good sound insulation
low dry specific density	=	good thermal insulation

Masonry standards: harmonized European product standard

The harmonized European product number series EN 771 (Specification for masonry units) is valid in the EU states. The series consists of:

EN 771-1 Clay masonry units
EN 771-2 Calcium silicate masonry units
EN 771-3 Aggregate concrete masonry units
EN 771-4 Autoclaved aerated concrete masonry units
EN 771-5 Manufactured stone masonry units (dense and lightweight masonry units)
EN 771-6 Natural stone masonry units

The standards establish basic specifications for source materials, manufacture, requirements, description and testing of masonry units. They do not fix precise sizes, nominal dimensions and angles. To be traded in Europe, construction products in these categories must carry the CE mark as a sign of compliance with the standards. Approval of products, and thus permission to use them, is still a national responsibility.

> 🛈

Clay masonry
units

STANDARD MASONRY UNITS

The clay brick is one of the oldest artificial building materials in the world. Bricks were made as long as 4000 years ago in the Haruppa cities on the Indus, and even then they had roughly the same dimensions and shape as today's standard brick. At first, mud bricks were baked in the sun, then the fired clay brick developed into a high-tech product, porous and thus offering excellent heat insulation when made with combustible aggregates, or protection against the elements when fired to the point of sintering; it gave us our current image of masonry. Its form, finish and material were developed even further, and now come in a wide variety of units, with form and performance fixed precisely by standards. The brick stands for both a long tradition of craftsmanship and a progressive and economical building material. It is made by mixing loam and clay, pressed and extruded as a ribbon, cut into appropriate sizes and fired.

The harmonized standard EN-771 makes a distinction between LD and HD bricks, and divides them into categories I and II, which fix a tolerance limit for maintaining compressive strength and thus quality. To be classified in category I the probability of deviating from the declared compressive strength must not be above 5%. All the rest of the units in category II are no longer accepted by the national standards.

LD bricks are used mainly by the internal loadbearing leaf of a twin-leaf structure or for rendered single-leaf masonry, as they have a low dry density (<1000 kg/m^3) and thus good thermal insulation properties. This is achieved by adding polystyrene beads or sawdust that burn when the brick is fired and leave tiny pores. They may be used only for masonry protected from penetrating water.

HD bricks with a gross dry density of >1000 kg/m^3 are suitable for both protected and unprotected masonry. This includes resistant units for the outer leaf and heavy sound-insulating units for the internal walls.

In these categories we distinguish:

Solid bricks	HD bricks with perpendicular perforation that takes up a maximum of 15% of the bed face or 20% of the volume.
Vertically perforated bricks	LD or HD bricks with vertical perforation of between 15% and 50% of the bed face. Here a distinction is made between perforation types A, B, C and W.
Heat insulation bricks	LD bricks with higher thermal insulation specifications and a special perforation type.
Solid vertically perforated facing bricks	A category of brick that is frost-resistant as well as meeting the above perforation specifications.
Solid and vertically perforated engineering bricks	HD bricks with a vitrified surface. They absorb only minimal quantities of water, have a compressive strength of at least class 28, are frost-resistant and have higher specific density requirements. Here a distinction is made according to the above-mentioned criteria between solid units and vertically perforated

Material:	Clay, loam, clayey masses		
Aggregates:	Sawdust, polystyrene beads (optional)		
Manufacture:	Moulded and fired		
Dimensions	In mm (e.g. 240 x 300 x 238) and in multiples of DF (e.g. 10DF)		
Unit types		Strength class*	Density class*
LD bricks	Vertically perforated brick	6–12	0.7–0.9
	Thermal insulation brick		
HD bricks	Solid brick	8–28 (36**)	1.6–2.2
	Vertically perforated brick	8–20 (36**)	1.2–1.6
	Solid facing brick	8–28 (36**)	1.8–2.2
	Vertically perforated facing brick	8–28 (36**)	1.2–1.6
	Solid engineering brick	28	1.8–2.2
	Vertically perforated engineering brick	28	1.8–2.2
	Solid engineering brick	60	1.8–2.2
	Vertically perforated high-strength engineering brick	60	1.8–2.2
	Panel brick		

* Common classes
** Values for high-strength bricks or engineering bricks (without special abbreviations)

units with holes A, B. C. High-strength engineering bricks must achieve a compressive strength of at least class 36.

High-strength engineering bricks
These have a compressive strength of at least class 60 and a specific density of 1.4. They are particularly resistant and durable.

Panel bricks
These have channels to take mortar or concrete when constructing reinforced masonry.

Additional stipulations concern the shape of grip openings that make the bricks easier to handle, or the form of mortar pockets or tongue and groove systems that work without visible mortar application to the perpends.

Calcium silicate units
Calcium silicate units have been made only since they were patented in 1880. Unlike bricks, they are not fired. Instead, a mixture of sand, water and lime is hardened under high pressure.

Fig.47:
Calcium silicate units

Table 3: Calcium silicate units			
Material:	Lime, sand (quartz sand), water		
Aggregates:	Dyes and additives		
Manufacture:	Mixed, moulded and hardened under pressure		
Dimensions	In mm (e.g. 240 x 300 x 238) and in multiples of DF (e.g. 10DF)		
Unit types		Strength class*	Density class*
	calcium silicate solid brick	12–28	1.6-2.0
	calcium silicate perforated / hollow block	12–20	1.2-1.6
	calcium silicate facing brick, solid brick	12–28	1.6-2.0
	calcium silicate facing brick, solid brick	20–28	1.6-2.0
	calcium silicate facing brick / perforated brick	12–20	1.4-1.6
	calcium silicate facing brick, perforated brick	20	1.4-1.6
	calcium silicate prefabricated bricks		
	calcium silicate prefabricated elements		

* Common classes

As for clay bricks, a distinction is made between solid calcium silicate bricks and perforated calcium bricks according to the proportion of holes: the upper limit is 15% of the bed face. Both sorts must have a unit height of less then 113 mm. Higher units are called calcium silicate blocks or hollow calcium silicate blocks. Calcium silicate facing bricks and calcium silicate engineering bricks are available for masonry exposed to weathering. Calcium silicate prefabricated bricks are available where appropriate for laying in thin-bed mortar and calcium silicate R units, which require no mortar for their perpends because of their tongue and groove system.

> see chapters Rules of construction, Finishing rules, and New approaches

Table 4:
Aerated and light concrete units

Material:	Lime, quartz sand, cement, water, expanding agent to form pores (aluminium)		
Aggregates:			
Manufacture:	Mixed, moulded and hardened under pressure		
Dimensions	In mm (e.g. 240 x 300 x 238)		
Unit types		Strength class*	Density class*
	Aerated concrete block unit	2-4	0.4-0.7
	Aerated concrete prefabricated unit	2-4	0.4-0.7
	Aerated concrete slab	Non-loadbearing	
	Prefabricated aerated concrete slab	Non-loadbearing	

* Common classes

Aerated
concrete units

This type was also developed in the late 19th century. For the manufacture of aerated concrete units, a mixture of quartz sand, lime and cement is poured moulds with water and provided with steel mesh reinforcement according to purpose. Powdered aluminium is used as an expanding agent, increasing the proportion of pores to 90% of the material's volume through the release of hydrogen. The unmoulded material is cut and hardened under pressure.

Porous concrete is like the natural mineral tobermorite and is offers high thermal and sound insulation because of its high porosity.

Large-format aerated concrete blocks or prefabricated units for thin-bed mortar are used for loadbearing walls.

Aerated concrete slabs and prefabricated slabs are used only for non-loadbearing walls with different loadbearing systems, and for sound insulation walls.

Fig.49:
Concrete and lightweight concrete units

Table 5: Concrete and lightweight concrete bricks and slabs			
Material:	Mineral aggregates and hydraulic binding agents		
Aggregates:	Pumice, expanded clay for lightweight concrete		
Manufacture:	Mixed, moulded		
Dimensions	In mm (e.g. 240 x 300 x 238) and in multiples of DF (e.g. 10DF)		
Brick types	Category	Strength class*	Density class*
	Concrete bricks		
	Solid concrete bricks	12-20	1.6-2.0
	Solid concrete bricks	12-20	1.6-2.0
	Hollow concrete bricks	2-12	0.8-1.4
	Concrete facing bricks	12-20	1.6-2.0
	Concrete facing block	12-20	1.6-2.0
	Lightweight concrete bricks		
	Solid lightweight concrete bricks	2-6	0.6-2.0
	Solid lightweight concrete blocks	12	1.6-2.0
	with slots		
	with slots and special thermal insulation properties		0.5-0.7**
	Prefabricated bricks		
	Hollow	2-6	0.5-0.7
	Lightweight concrete wall elements	Non-loadbearing	
	Hollow lightweight concrete wall elements	Non-loadbearing	

* Common classes
** Standard specification – to clarify special thermal insulation properties

Storey-height elements and ceiling slabs complete the product programme as additions to classical masonry construction.

Concrete and lightweight concrete units

Concrete and lightweight concrete units are cast in moulds and stored until they reach their ultimate strength. The difference between the two lies in the nature of the aggregates. Only lightweight aggregates with a porous microstructure (primarily natural pumice or expanded clay) may be used for lightweight concrete.

A distinction is made here in terms of dimensions as well as aggregates. Solid bricks are limited to a height of 115 mm, which distinguishes them from solid blocks, which are 175 mm or 238 mm high. Neither type is permitted to have cells, but only grip openings. Hollow blocks with a preferred height of 238 mm do have cells, whose number precedes the unit category (e.g. 3K). Facing units or facing blocks must be used in situations with weathering.

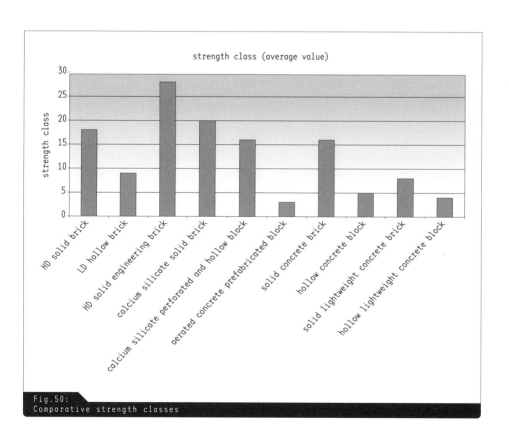

Fig.50:
Comparative strength classes

63

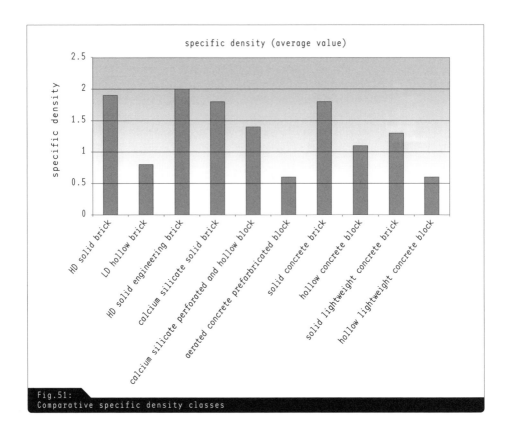

specific density (average value)

Fig.51:
Comparative specific density classes

Lightweight concrete units are distinguished according to the same criteria between solid bricks, solid blocks and hollow blocks. There are also bricks with slots and special insulating properties, identified by the endings -S or -SW, and prefabricated bricks.

Lightweight concrete wall construction elements and hollow wall elements are manufactured for non-loadbearing walls.

> ⚲
> \\ Important:
> Site-mixed mortar is not covered by European standards. National user or working standards must be consulted here.

Mortar type Abbreviations according to EN 998-2	Mortar class according to EN 998-2 (only CE sign)	Forms available
Normal-weight mortar (G)		Premixed dry mortar Ready-mixed mortar Multi-chamber silo mortar (building site mortars in Germany)
	M2,5	
	M5	
	M10	
	M15	
	M30	
Lightweight mortar L		Premixed dry mortar Ready-mixed mortar Multi-chamber silo mortar
	M10	
	M10	
Thin-bed mortar T		Premixed dry mortar
	M15	

TYPES OF MORTAR FOR MASONRY

Mortar is made up of binding agents, admixtures and additives. Admixtures affect mortar properties such as frost resistance or workability, and may be added in larger quantities. Additives change the properties of the mortar through chemical and physical processes and may be used to a limited extent only. They include liquefiers, retarders and air entrainers. The components are supplied either individually and mixed on site (site-mixed mortar), or are delivered to the site ready-mixed.

All the components except the water can be supplied ready-mixed (premixed dry mortar), or to save time the ready-made mortar can be supplied to the site from the factory. Retarders allow for the necessary working time (ready-mixed mortar). For premixed dry mortar, only the non-hardening materials are mixed, so water and cement have to be added on site. One variant of ready-mixed mortar is supplied as multi-chamber silo mortar. Here the components are mixed on site as well, but without the possibility of altering the mixing ratio.

\\ Important:
Similarly to bricks, the national standards
DIN V 20000-412 (user standard) and DIN 18580
(residual standard) apply additionally in
Germany. But essentially the specifications of
DIN 1053-1 still apply.

\\ Important:
Masonry mortars show considerable
discrepancies between the European standard
and the stipulations of DIN 1053 in Germany.
Here precise attention must be paid to the
user and residual standards!

> ♀ Just like masonry units, mortar for masonry is subject to precisely specified manufacture, inspection, categorization and property definition. The harmonized product standard DIN EN 998-2 applies in the EU.

This divides masonry mortar into three types: normal-weight mortar (G), lightweight mortar (L) and thin-bed mortar (T).

Normal-weight mortar differs from lightweight mortar in terms of its dry gross density m, which must be at least 1500 kg/m^3, while lightweight mortar has a dry density of less than 1300 kg/m^3. Thin-bed mortar was developed specially for gauged bricks and reduces the mortar height to 1–3 mm. Here the dry density may not be less than 1500 kg/m^3 and the maximum aggregate particle size is 2 mm. All mortar types are allocated to the mortar groups M1–M30 according to their compressive strength; the compressive strength value is given in N/mm^2. If a mortar complies with

> ♀ DIN EN 998-2 it is marked with the CE sign.

IN CONCLUSION

The information contained in this book can give only a rough guide to the many possibilities offered by masonry construction. For this reason, it does not generally cover the regulations laid down in the different national standards, which sometimes differ. These will have to be addressed separately, using the list of standards in the Appendix. But the knowledge presented does provide the necessary basis for understanding the essential rules of the craft and the areas in which masonry is used, and makes it possible for the reader to continue independently.

Many regular constructions can be explored using the principles shown in the second chapter, which present an extensive design repertoire for the planner. The constructions listed in the third will make it easier to put the legal rulings and standards in context. Problems arising from related topics such concrete construction or façades, or more advanced expositions of structural behaviour or building science, will be more readily understood. Information from manufacturers and dealers, which the internet is turning into an increasingly wide and important reference source for planners, is made easier to filter by the details given in the fourth chapter, when making selections for future building commissions.

All in all, these "Basics" make it possible to explore the diverse world of masonry construction and approach it correctly.

APPENDIX

STANDARDS

Masonry units:

EN 771-1 (consult national versions)	Specifications for bricks – Part 1: Clay masonry units
EN 771-2 (consult national versions)	Specifications for bricks – Part 2: Calcium silicate masonry units
EN 771-3 (consult national versions)	Specifications for bricks – Part 3: Aggregate concrete masonry units (dense and lightweight aggregates)
EN 771-4 (consult national versions)	Specifications for bricks – Part 4: Autoclaved aerated concrete masonry units
EN 771-5 (consult national versions)	Specifications for bricks – Part 5: Manufactured stone masonry units
EN 771-6 (consult national versions)	Specifications for bricks – Part 6: Natural stone masonry units

Masonry mortar:

EN 998-2 (consult national versions)	Specifications for mortar in masonry structures – Part 2: Masonry mortar

Other building parts and materials:

EN 845-1 (consult national versions)	Specifications for additional parts for masonry – Part 1: Anchors, tie members, bearings and brackets

Loads and forces:

EN V 1996-1-1	Eurocode 6: Dimensioning and constructing masonry buildings Part 1-1: General rules – rules for reinforced and non-reinforced masonry

LITERATURE

Andrea Deplazes (ed.): *Constructing Architecture*, Birkhäuser Publishers, Basel 2005

Francis D.K. Ching: *Building Construction illustrated*, 3rd edition, John Wiley & Sons, 2004

Ernst Neufert, Peter Neufert: *Architects' Data*, 3rd edition, Blackwell Science, UK USA Australia 2004

Andrew Watts: *Modern Construction Roofs*, Springer, Wien New York 2006

Günter Pfeifer, Rolf Ramcke, Joachim Achtziger, Konrad Zilch: *Masonry Construction Manual*, Birkhäuser Publishers, Basel 2001

Jacques Heyman: *The Stone Skeleton: Stuctural Engineering of Masonry Architecture*, Cambridge University Press, Cambridge 1995

Theodor Hugues, Klaus Greilich, Christine Peter: *Detail Practice: Building with Large Clay Blocks and Panels*, Birkhäuser Publishers, Basel 2005

Construction Products Directive: Directive of the Council of 21 December 1988 (89/106/EEC)

Kenneth Burke: *Perspectives by Incongruity*, Indiana University Press, Bloomington 1964

Andrea Palladio: *I Quattro Libri dell' Architettura*, English translation by Robert Tavernor, MIT Press, Cambridge, Massachusetts 1997

Series editor: Bert Bielefeld
Conception: Bert Bielefeld, Annette Gref

Layout and Cover design: Muriel Comby
Translation into English: Michael Robinson
English Copy editing: Monica Buckland

Quotation page 7: Detail Review of Architecture,
10/2005, Munich, page 1066

A CIP catalogue record for this book is available
from the Library of Congress, Washington D.C.,
USA

Bibliographic information published by
Die Deutsche Bibliothek
Die Deutsche Bibliothek lists this publication in
the Deutsche Nationalbibliografie; detailed
bibliographic data is available on the Internet at
http://dnb.ddb.de.

This book is also available in a German (ISBN 3-
7643-7643-0) and a French (ISBN 3-7643-7955-3)
language edition.

© 2007 Birkhäuser – Publishers for Architecture,
P.O. Box 133, CH-4010 Basel, Switzerland
Member of Springer Science + Business Media

Printed on acid-free paper produced from
chlorine-free pulp. TCF ∞
Printed in Germany

ISBN-10: 3-7643-7645-7
ISBN-13: 978-3-7643-7645-1
9 8 7 6 5 4 3 2 1   www.birkhauser.ch

ALSO AVAILABLE FROM BIRKHÄUSER:

Basics Design and Housing
Jan Krebs
ISBN 3-7643-7647-3

Basics Materiality
Manfred Hegger, Hans Drexler, Martin Zeumer
ISBN 3-7643-7685-6

Basics Modelbuilding
Alexander Schilling
ISBN 3-7643-7649-X

Basics Technical Drawing
Bert Bielefeld, Isabella Skiba
ISBN 3-7643-7644-9

Basics Roof Construction
Tanja Brotrück
ISBN 3-7643-7683-X